TESTIMONIALS

I've known Jeff Levin for forty years, and his entrepreneurial spirit continues to impress me. His track record demonstrates a real expertise in earning excess returns. In our current environment of higher risk and lower expected investment returns, the road map of private lending he lays out in *The Insider's Guide to Private Lending* is of great value to nearly all investors.

—Craig Peterman, CFA, CFP®, Managing Director, Prism Wealth Management

I have known Jeff Levin for years and thoroughly enjoyed reading *The Insider's Guide to Private Lending*. Levin is a key player in the private lending space and is someone to listen to. His stories lay out many of the dos and don'ts in private lending.

—Anthony Geraci, Esquire, Geraci Law Firm

Jeff Levin is an industry leader and his most recent offering, *The Insider's Guide to Private Lending*, provides a great overview of the industry while teaching many important lessons.

—Joel Block, CEO, Bullseye Capital

Jeff Levin is an expert in his area. He is our go-to person to review real estate investment opportunities and the various financing options of our projects, large and small. Levin has developed his private money lending business with a keen sense of the financial market, knowledge of real estate trends, and his ability to build on relationships. Not only does he know the basics of private money lending, inside and out, but he provides creative solutions to complicated financial situations others may not clearly understand.

Private money is all about relationships, creativity, and trust. Jeff Levin is the epitome of all three and with *The Insider's Guide to Private Lending,* his reach will help to guide many new and experienced private money lenders and real estate investors on the right path to financial growth.

—Linda McElligott, Real Estate Investor

THE INSIDER'S GUIDE TO PRIVATE LENDING

THE INSIDER'S GUIDE TO PRIVATE LENDING

JEFF LEVIN

Private Lending Publications

The Insider's Guide to Private Lending

Published by Private Lending Publications

Copyright © 2018 by Jeff Levin

All rights reserved.

Private Lending Publications
503 Independence Ave SE
Washington, DC 20003
Email: info@privatelendingpublications.com
Phone: (202) 503-4065

Limit of Liability/Disclaimer of Warranty:

Publishing and editorial team:
Author Bridge Media, www.AuthorBridgeMedia.com
Project Manager and Editorial Director: Helen Chang
Editor: Katherine MacKenett
Publishing Manager: Laurie Aranda
Publishing Assistant: Iris Sasing
Cover design: Deb Tremper

Library of Congress Control Number: 2017954995
ISBN: 978-0-9994230-0-4 -- softcover
978-0-9994230-2-8 -- hardback
978-0-9994230-1-1 -- ebook

Ordering Information:

Quantity sales. Special discounts are available on quantity purchases by corporations, associations, and others. For details, contact the publisher at the address above.

Printed in the United States of America

DEDICATION

To my children, Jack and Charlie—you are my pride, my joy, my love.

To my wife, Dunnzy Kaufman Levin—thank you for all that you do for me and for loving me.

To my parents, Lloyd and Sheri Levin—your guidance and love made me who I am today.

Acknowledgments

As with all things worthwhile, there are many people who contribute to the outcome. This book is no different and would not have happened without the support and encouragement of many people in my life.

While several people contributed to this effort, I would like to thank the following individuals who played a direct role in helping me to develop and complete this book.

First and foremost, a special thank you to Helen Chang, Katherine MacKenett, Jenny Shipley, and the entire team at Author Bridge Media. While one may have the idea and desire to write a book, the process of writing one is a whole different story. Thank you all for your editorial and publishing services. You kept us on track and asked insightful questions that stimulated additional ideas and helped add clarity and depth to the text.

Thank you to my dad—without your help and guidance, this book would not have been written or finished. Your mentorship and encouragement continue to enable me to pursue my dreams.

Thank you to Tabitha Fitzgerald, my business confidante and advisor. You played a key role in inspiring me to write this book and have stuck with me through all of the success stories, as well as the lessons learned.

Thank you to David Coutoumanos—your help and organization have been the backbone of this effort.

A sincere thank you to Lisa Gans; you are a leader of leaders. Your guidance and friendship were integral to my making it over the finish line.

Finally, thank you to my wife, Dunnzy. Without your help, this book would not have come to fruition. Your love, support, and vision continue to keep me grounded in everything that I pursue.

CONTENTS

INTRODUCTION

Becoming a private lender can be a leap into the unknown. There is great potential for high returns and quick cycles, but with the excitement and reward come risks and the possibility of failure and loss. Between a lender and success, there is a maze of connections, decisions, regulations, and processes that need to be navigated successfully. While there will always be things beyond any lender's control, through experience, or learning from the experiences of others, you can mitigate the risk and set yourself up to succeed as a private lender.

My Personal Plunge

My experience in private lending has taught me many lessons. In writing this book, I hope to share my experiences with those just starting out so that newcomers to the space can benefit. Over the years, I have developed my own "system"—basically an approach and a set of principles, guidelines, rules, and processes—that allows me to achieve more success than failure. I am writing this book with the hope that this guide will help you to master some of the secrets and avoid many of the potential pitfalls of private lending.

My own journey began with a toe-dip into the private lending waters. Though I had spent more than twenty-five years working for and building mortgage companies, and had flipped properties and bought others to hold, I had never used my own money to make a loan. However, as a mortgage broker, I noticed that the process of getting a loan for an investment property was difficult and time consuming, and was becoming more so. After years of watching borrowers struggle with the process, in 2007, I finally had the chance to step in and fill that growing gap in the market by making a private loan.

That year, I sold one of the properties that I had bought to hold, and suddenly I had $500,000 in cash to lend. So, I began making small loans to people looking for short-term capital. Some of the loans were successful and others were not, but I found that I was learning from each transaction. Even after several profitable loans, I still viewed these deals as side projects. My father, Lloyd, who is also a real estate entrepreneur, suggested, "Jeff, you're always getting phone calls from people who want to borrow money. Why don't you become a private lender full time?" I realized that I really enjoyed earning a living by supporting others in their projects, but I still hesitated to make the leap.

Then, in 2008, the Great Recession hit, and it turned the mortgage business upside down. More stringent regulations and the decline of values in the real estate market created new difficulties, and traditional mortgage lenders saw their business shrink as scrutiny of borrowers heightened. But, because of my foray into private lending, I saw an opportunity in all of the disruption. I realized that there were many qualified borrowers who were being turned away as banks pulled back. The restriction of traditional lending platforms, coupled with the opportunity to buy distressed properties for a fraction of their former value, created a major gap in the lending market that was begging to be filled.

That year, I made a loan to an accountant who also saw the decline in real estate values as an opportunity. She wanted to buy during the market dip and continue to build her rental portfolio. She had excellent credit and more than a $1 million net worth, and yet her bank had turned her down for a loan. So, I agreed to lend to her. She renovated the property within sixty days and had it rented and then refinanced within a four-month period. During her refinance, she was able to recoup her down payment and have passive positive cash flow of $1,000 per month. I realized that in filling this gap in the market, I was able to supplement my income as the mortgage lending business declined, while simultaneously helping people who had no other access to capital make successful investments and leverage the opportunities that the recession had created in order to turn a profit. In fact, most of my early borrowers were people making modest investments and slowly building up their portfolios, rather than established real estate professionals.

I really enjoyed the experience of making a loan to a borrower that allowed us both to thrive. In the Jewish prayer book *Pirkei Avot*, Rabbi Hillel says, "If I am not for myself, who will be for me? But if I am only for myself, who am I? If not now, when?" I believe in making the world a better place, and not just for me. I've had the opportunity to do that for many of my borrowers, and now, I hope to do that by helping others succeed in private lending by sharing my knowledge and learnings.

Over the years, I have met many wonderful people in private lending and have often received genuinely helpful support and advice. Looking back now, I realize that I could have benefited from having more mentors and better strategies. My goal in this book is to set out my own system, and share advice I've received along the way, to help you.

Who Can Benefit from This Book?

This book is meant to help anyone who is considering private lending as part of a balanced portfolio, as well as those with a bit more knowledge about real estate who may be looking to launch their own private lending businesses. You may be a baby boomer with a fair amount of money in your retirement account, looking for new ways to diversify or increase returns. Or you may have generational money to put to work and want to find new investment opportunities. Or, you may have experience purchasing and flipping properties but never have considered lending to others.

Whatever your current circumstance is, you have money. You want to invest it. But you are not quite sure how to invest in real estate, and whether it's a viable option for your portfolio. You may have thought about becoming a rehabber, but you recognize that it is a full-time job. Buying and holding rental properties seems safe—but you don't want to fix toilets, and it takes too long to get a payoff. You may even be a mortgage broker or real estate agent who sees what's going on in the market and wants to learn how to put your own capital to work. Whether private lending is a new idea for you or something you've been interested in for a while, I hope to be able to provide you with the opportunity to learn more and identify private lending opportunities that are right for you.

Five Benefits of Private Lending

When you understand how to do it right, private lending is a powerful tool that can help you achieve stellar returns while minimizing your risk—without lifting a hammer, repairing a tenant's toilet, or showing houses. I believe that private lending should be a part of any well-diversified portfolio. Here are five good reasons why:

1. Returns

As a private lender, you provide a unique service. Typically, you act more quickly than a bank will and provide more flexibility in your requirements and process. For that additional benefit and convenience, your borrowers are willing to pay you a premium. This premium can be up to double or triple what banks charge on traditional home loans. When you learn how to mitigate the risks of lending, it can become an engine for healthy returns.

2. Convenience

One way that individuals have made money in real estate is by flipping properties. There are many advantages to sweat equity, but it's time consuming, and not everyone has the skill set to do it. Private lending allows individual investors to benefit from lucrative real estate projects without an investment of extensive time or construction expertise.

3. Diversification

While some private lenders choose to fund a project in its entirety, other spread their dollars over a portfolio of several flips at a time, allowing them to spread their risk while still benefiting from high rates of return. If you decide to fund only part of a loan, you should be aware that there are different capital structures when more than one lender is involved, so it's important to understand and negotiate the loan terms that work best for you.

4. Protection from Market Volatility

The average private lending transaction generally spans a period of three to twelve months, during which your money goes out and comes back, yielding interest. While the stock market is vulnerable to dramatic short-term swings, often as a result of events and forces beyond your control, the conditions in the short-term real estate market remain relatively stable, and you have the ability to mitigate the risks in the deal through your process and decisions. By carefully selecting and vetting your borrowers, electing favorable terms that fit the needs of your portfolio, and lending for short windows, you can shield yourself from the volatility that is inherent in so many other investment vehicles.

5. Pacing

Another advantage to private lending is that you can invest at a gradual pace, one that feels comfortable to you. You can start with one simple loan and enjoy the stream of income coming in from that one loan until it's paid off. You can then take the profit from that first loan and invest in two deals, then three, and soon you will have a predictable income. That income can even be tax-free if you invest through a self-directed IRA, leaving you with potentially sizable gains in the long run.

In this book, I'll explain more about how to make money as a private lender and describe a number of ways to enter the private lending market. I hope you'll find a path that is right for you.

Chapter 1

WHAT IS PRIVATE LENDING?

The Gold Rush

The opportunities presented by private lending are like those presented by the California gold rush. Imagine you hear the call: "They found gold out West!" You head to California to try your luck. You try panning for gold, looking for flakes and nuggets in the rivers.

All around you, you see other people on the same quest. And though many do find a golden nugget, not all of them will. Then you take a closer look, and you notice that there are a few people who are making a consistent profit. These are the merchants and businesspeople servicing the gold-mining towns. The merchants don't have gold, but they have what every miner needs. They supply tools, provide transportation, and sell clothes, food, and drinks.

Though not searching for gold, these entrepreneurs are very much a part of the gold rush. Rather than searching for a big score, they earn their money slowly and steadily by servicing the miners, just as we service those who want to undertake real estate transactions. This is what private lending is all about.

What Is Private Lending?

Private lending is not a get-rich-quick scheme. So . . . what is it?

Private lending is simply a private individual or organization making a loan to another individual or company in the real estate profession. Private lenders, sometimes referred to as "hard money lenders," make short-term loans, usually to short-term fix-and-flippers, as well as long-term investors, looking for quick funding to rehab or purchase a property, which will later be financed by a more traditional long-term lender.

Private loans are backed by an asset, such as a piece of real estate that someone is looking to finance. The borrower receives a loan secured by the value of that collateral, meaning that if the borrower is unable to repay the loan, the lender may foreclose on the property and use it to settle the balance owed by the borrower. The interest rates for a private loan are typically higher than those offered by banks or traditional financing institutions because of the risk-reward ratio involved.

As a private lender, you can make money in three ways. First, you can charge an origination fee. This is a fee your borrower pays to borrow the money. Second, you collect interest monthly on the loan. And finally, in some cases, you can charge an exit fee, which is a fee due from the borrower when the loan is paid off.

Private lending, if you do it correctly, is one of the best ways to earn a relatively safe, higher rate of return on your money. Instead of investing in stocks and bonds, you have a tangible asset that serves as collateral for your loan. And because you are taking more risk than banks, which can be heavily regulated, and which generally have a more time-consuming and stringent underwriting process, the interest rates you can charge as a private lender are often far above market—anywhere between 5 percent and 15 percent annually per loan.

There are many reasons why people come to private lenders. In real estate, your borrowers are often rehabbers who are fixing and flipping properties. Rehabbers need to close deals quickly with motivated house sellers. This means they typically make purchase offers to pay all cash, buy as is, and close in as little as seven days. Often, banks can't make lending decisions that quickly, leaving the rehabber vulnerable to losing the opportunity to buy the property.

And sometimes, conventional banks won't lend on a highly distressed property because of the neighborhood in which it's located, the fact that the property is not generating cash flow in its current condition, or even the size of the loan. Occasionally, banks even turn down the most qualified borrowers with little or no explanation. And, because banks often refuse to lend for both the purchase price and the cost of a rehab, borrowers need alternate lending sources that will allow them to complete their projects.

These rehabbers turn to private lenders as an alternative solution when a conventional loan is not available. Private lenders—like you and me—can offer quick loans to buy and rehab a house, and in return for our speed and flexibility, we earn a higher rate of return than other investment vehicles offer.

Managing Risk in Your Lending Portfolio

When I was younger, I played baseball. As a baseball player, I thought that you always had to try to knock it out of the park. But in private lending, I don't always aim for a home run. My strategy has often been to hit singles and doubles over and over again. First base might be a 6 to 8 percent return on investment. Second base would be 8 to 12 percent. And while a home run could yield 13 percent or more, I take on those types of loans only under carefully controlled circumstances, because those rates of return generally come with much greater risk.

By focusing on incremental gains rather than seeking that big nugget of gold, you are much more likely to earn a consistent stream of interest income that can grow each time it is reinvested. In private lending, money is made transaction after transaction after transaction. The long-term gain comes from the income compounding and earning money, time and time again.

Over time, I have also learned to diversify my lending portfolio, with respect to both projects and borrowers, to make sure that I'm not too heavily invested in one project, or with one borrower across projects. In the beginning of my private lending career, I made four loans to one borrower within thirty days. Each transaction made sense: all of the loans were for good projects, and the borrower was very experienced and had a large rental portfolio and net worth. But, after I made the loans, I realized that my concentration with this borrower was too high.

At the time, I had $1 million to lend and had loaned almost $300,000 of it to this borrower. If something had happened to my borrower's projects, my portfolio would have suffered a major setback. Fortunately, he paid off all of the loans, and I have since limited my concentration per borrower. I am careful to make sure that no one borrower makes up more than 10 to 15 percent of my overall lending portfolio.

An Evolving Industry

The private lending industry is one of the oldest industries, and yet, like most industries, it is constantly evolving.

Modern private lending has been significantly reshaped by the Great Recession of 2008, which altered the perspective of conventional lenders. In its aftermath, the regulatory landscape also tightened. A new set of rules was created for banks, and new regulatory bodies, such as the Consumer Financial Protection Bureau, set out explicit rules governing banks' lending processes and decisions.

This additional scrutiny also came with new penalties for lax lending practices. The cost of complying with the new regulations actually has led some banks to cut back on their traditional mortgage lending businesses completely. And because there was a crackdown on lending to borrowers with low FICO credit scores, it has become increasingly difficult for individuals with sound flipping opportunities who lack perfect credit histories to secure loans.

This new reality for conventional lenders and real estate borrowers has created immense opportunity for private lenders, and an array of these less-regulated institutions and individuals has emerged to fill the gap left by traditional lenders. While there continue to be changes in the space, including the potential for a relaxation of the ties that currently bind traditional lenders, this period of increased market share for private lenders has allowed more borrowers to become comfortable working with private lenders and has contributed to an expansion and maturation of the private lending industry.

Before You Start

You may be asking, "How do I know if private lending is right for me?"

To answer that, you may want to look at the different entry points into the field and decide which one is most comfortable for you. The factors that should influence your answer include the amount of capital you have to invest, your level or expertise, and your risk tolerance.

The next question is, "How much money do I need to get started?"

The answer to this will depend on the market you are in and how you choose to participate. Five thousand dollars can be enough to get involved with certain projects in some markets. However, for more meaningful investing, the magic number is at least $50,000. That amount, invested at an average rate of 8 percent and compounded annually, will be worth just over $233,000 in twenty years.

Finally, you want to ask, "Do I have the resources and knowledge I need to dive into private lending?" As with all meaningful investments, you will want to make sure that your interests and your investments are protected. As I will discuss in the next chapter, there are many ways to deploy your capital as a private lender. The more directly you are involved in the vetting and underwriting of loans, the more expertise you'll require. Part of my hope in writing this book is to help you identify resources and professionals who can help you along your journey, so that you can find your niche and be successful in it.

The Road Map

If you know you are ready to explore private lending seriously, this book can serve as your initial map. Each chapter is a stop on the highway toward your ultimate destination of being a private lender. No matter how you ultimately choose to participate in the space, this book will help you understand the six stops in a private lending transaction, from finding the opportunity to getting paid.

> *How to find opportunities.* If you don't find lending opportunities in the first place, you can't invest in them. I'll show you how and where to find people who need money for their real estate projects—money that you can supply.

> *Who to lend to.* As the saying goes, you want to know who you're getting into bed with. Becoming familiar with the person you are going to lend your money to is one of the most important ways to mitigate your risk.

> *What kind of property to invest in.* It is important to know the value of the asset you are lending on so that you can structure an appropriate loan.

This is key to being successful as a private lender. You can use many different tools to assess the value of a piece of real estate, and I'll help you understand them.

When to make a loan. You have to evaluate each transaction properly and in the same way every time, no matter the amount of the loan. Following the rules that you set up for every loan will give you security. Evaluating a deal correctly will allow you to understand when to make a loan and when to take a pass. You also need to have at least one exit strategy that allows you to achieve the outcome you and your borrower desire, and it's always good to have a back-up plan.

How to protect yourself and your investment. It's important to avail yourself of all opportunities to mitigate risk and secure your investment. You want to be certain you've properly assessed the value of your collateral. You want to insure your loans. You also want to make sure that your documents are recorded correctly. I'll help you understand how to protect your loans and who you should turn to for needed support along the way.

How to get paid. This is what private lending is all about. To get paid, you need to know how to service the loan. You also need to keep track of each loan and know when to collect payment, and you must monitor and follow up with your borrowers on a regular basis. I'll walk you through this process to help you understand the mechanics of turning a profit.

Remember the California gold rush. In the next chapter, we'll look at the different ways you can lend to the miners and build up your experience so that you can even begin to identify which miners are likely to be successful and worth cultivating as repeat clients.

Chapter 2

How to Find Opportunities

On-Ramps to Private Lending

When I began making private loans, I was already a mortgage broker, and I had years of personal experience in buying and flipping properties. So, when I started lending, I already had many of the pieces that I needed to jump into the deep end of the pool and take on the entire lending process. But it's important to remember that you don't have to jump in all at once. There are many ways to get started, and you can find the right level of support, no matter what your level of expertise.

Private lending is a boutique business, and no two deals are ever exactly the same. There are also many different paths and levels of participation for lenders. If you're new to the space, make sure to look at all of your options. Here are five different ways to make private loans, each requiring different levels of capital and expertise.

1. Online Lending Platforms

If you're just starting out, don't have a lot to invest—say, $5,000 to $10,000—or just want the opportunity to spread your capital among a range of real estate projects, consider investing through an online real estate crowdfunding platform. These platforms, such as Fundrise, Realty Mogul, RealtyShares, or Prodigy Network, offer the opportunity for investors to pick from a range of investments and property types in a variety of locations. All of the opportunities featured have been underwritten by the platforms, so you will have experts vetting the deals that are offered before they go online. Generally, these sites are available only to accredited investors, though a few have offered opportunities that are more widely available. Rates of return on these deals can range from 5 percent up to 20 percent.

2. Experienced Private Lenders

Many private lenders accept capital from investors. Often, experienced lenders have great demand for loans. This demand may exceed their capital capacity, and they often are willing to accept money from investors, which they then place into their deals. These lenders have the industry knowledge and underwriting infrastructure in place and are often willing to engage with their investors about how they'll deploy their funds. This can be an excellent way for new investors to learn more about the process and is also a way to diversify a portfolio without having to take on too much of the lending process. I have investors who regularly place their money with me, and I've been able to help them find deals that meet their investing needs.

3. Loans to Friends and Family

Often, lenders who are just starting out make loans to people they know well. These deals can provide an opportunity for a new lender to stay close to the process once the flip begins and to build up lending experience. In these cases, it's important to make sure that the loan won't affect the relationship and to talk through, ahead of time, what will happen if the project runs into difficulty. No one wants to foreclose on mom or Aunt Edith!

4. Start a Self-Directed IRA

A self-directed IRA can be a traditional or a Roth IRA. It permits a wide range of investments not available with other retirement vehicles, including real estate investments. Using a self-directed IRA, you can buy, sell, or flip properties; redirect funds from one project to another; and lend to real estate flippers while deferring tax payments on gains. Essentially, as a private lender with a self-directed IRA, you conduct all of your lending activities through the

IRA and accrue your profits on a tax-deferred basis. You can do as much or as little lending as suits your portfolio and set your own pace, as part of a retirement savings plan. Self-directed IRAs are managed by a custodian—generally a company that holds the assets and approves investments. The custodian can help you make sure that you comply with all of the IRS requirements so that you are able to maintain your investments' tax-deferred status.

5. A Private Lending LLC

If you have both the industry knowledge and the time, you may want to launch your own private lending firm, the way that I have. If you take this route, you'll be responsible for generating lending opportunities, managing your own underwriting process, and selecting the degree of risk and potential upside that works for you. If you choose this path, you'll need to understand the entire cycle of a deal, beginning with that initial lead and ending with a final payoff of the loan. The rest of this chapter will help you learn more about what it takes to generate lending opportunities, and the rest of the book will take you through the cycle of a loan. In addition, there are courses offered by the National Private Lending Institute, through the American Association of Private Lenders (AAPL), that you can take to help you develop a much deeper understanding of private lending transactions and become an accredited private lender. You can also attend conferences, such as the AAPL's, Leonard Rosen's Pitbull Conference, the Geraci Conference Series, and the Think Realty Conference, where you can learn more and begin networking.

The Ocean City Convention

If you decide to make the leap and become a private lender, the first step is to find opportunities to lend. Since 2003, my colleagues and I have attended a real estate convention in Ocean City, Maryland. For years, nothing came of it, but we kept going. We always made an array of contacts at the conference, but initially, we didn't see any direct benefit to our business from attending.

One of the acquaintances I made at the conference is a man named Shawn. Shawn's earnings had been cut in half after the Great Recession, and when I met him in 2008, he expressed interest in becoming a house flipper to generate additional income. We talked more, and I discovered that he was a really wonderful, entrepreneurial guy, but at the time he was not quite ready to begin flipping properties. Still, I looked forward to seeing him every year.

In 2012, after we had known each other for several years, Shawn made the leap into real estate flipping and became one of my borrowers. For his first flip, I loaned him $156,000, which he turned into a profit of $75,000, and on which I earned $10,000. Since then, Shawn and I have done more than thirty-five single-family fix-and-flip transactions together. His loans with me have totaled in the millions of dollars, and I've made more than 15 percent on the capital loaned. Shawn could go to a bank at any time, but he prefers to come to me because it's easy and we have an established relationship.

Over the years, Shawn has become a friend, as well as one of my best clients. And the business I've done with this one person alone has covered the cost of attending that conference all those years several times over. So, my advice to you is to invest in networking and to be patient if leads don't seem to materialize immediately. Building a reputation and a network of borrowers takes time, but once you find quality borrowers, they will generate a stream of referrals, and your pipeline for opportunities will begin to support itself.

Always Be Networking

Finding deals consists of three steps: First, you have to put yourself in the right places. Then you have to know how to evaluate the people you meet. And finally, you have to build relationships. How do you put yourself in the right situation to encounter transactions that might be worthy of a private loan? Simply put: Always Be Networking.

Spend your time connecting with people who are likely to be seeking loans or those who work with potential borrowers. Real estate professionals, developers, and flippers are all good sources for opportunities. Real estate markets are regional, so focus on getting to know the real estate community in your area. Real estate meet-ups are held all the time all over the country for people to talk about a wide range of real estate topics. These are people with similar interests who want to talk about investing, borrowing, and lending. If you have any connections to professionals who are active in the real estate market, ask them for an introduction.

If you don't have personal connections to tap, sign up for a real estate conference or go online. The internet is a big place. You can find a lot of different people with a range of interests, and some of those people will need what you have to offer. Once you have made some connections, you will want to stay plugged in to that community. You can schedule follow-up coffee meetings, golf games, or dinners. Remember, you find transactions by meeting people, so networking is the best way to gain access to potential lending opportunities.

Reputation Is Key

How do you build a reputation as a trustworthy private lender? The most important thing is to behave reputably. Private lending takes place within the context of a community, and members of that community talk to each other.

As you complete more and more transactions, people will begin to know you and refer borrowers to you.

This does not happen instantly. Completing your first loan successfully will provide you with a reference for your second potential borrower to call. You want that person to be able to verify that you did what you promised when it was promised, and that the loan process was a success. After your second, third, and fourth successfully completed loans, you will have both a resume and a core group of borrowers who can confirm that you are a reliable and trustworthy private lender.

I always try to work with my borrowers, to understand their goals, and to help them achieve them. It is this, more than anything, that has helped my reputation. I once made a $2 million loan to a borrower. He came to me just as the loan was coming due, saying that he needed an additional three weeks to pay off the balance. At the time, it was the largest loan I had ever made, and I was pleased to be making a hefty return. Our agreement would have allowed me to charge an additional 10 percent on the loan during his requested extension period, but I wanted to end the transaction on a high note, so I charged only a nominal 1 percent for those final three weeks. My borrower felt supported in what could have been a stressful situation and, as a result, referred many other clients to me. These referrals have generated more in profits than I would have made on that one extension had I decided to charge the maximum to which I was entitled under the agreement.

Building your brand as a lender within a community is reinforced by your conduct and your networking. The connections that you make to build relationships, get deals, and find opportunities will create a buzz. Remember that strong relationships are built around trust, integrity, and rapport, and that, as you nurture your relationships, you will find more and more transactions, which in turn will allow you to grow your business.

Finding the Right Borrowers

Everybody in the real estate industry is looking for money. Banks, developers, equity providers, and even investors are looking to bring more economic leverage to the table in order to tackle different transactions. So, when you are networking, how do you filter potential borrowers?

The first thing I want to find out when I speak to potential borrowers is how much experience they have. I also inquire about the types of transactions they have done and whether those transactions were recent. This information helps me evaluate whether they know what a good deal is and whether their skills and experience are up to date. In the past, I've learned a lot about potential borrowers by engaging with them and asking them questions about their past, but it is important to remember that initial impressions are no substitute for thorough investigation. For our next stop on the private lending journey, in chapter 3, I will explain in greater detail how to vet potential borrowers.

Chapter 3

WHO TO LEND TO

Russian Caviar

Before deciding to loan your money to someone, it is important to know who you are lending to.

In 2011, a man I met asked me for a loan. He had the requisite experience, and I liked him personally. I was inclined to do the transaction. Although everything looked good, I always do a background check before lending to anybody, and I did my homework in this case too.

It turned out that sticking to my process was a good thing. The criminal background check revealed that this potential borrower had once run a caviar smuggling ring. He had brought the caviar into the United States with labels forged to look as if the product had come from a legitimate supplier. Further research revealed that he had even bribed people to get permits to get the caviar into the United States.

I always try to give people the benefit of the doubt, but it's important to protect your business and to go through every step of the vetting process. In this case, not only was the potential borrower not as honest as he appeared, but he had actually been convicted of fraud. If I hadn't taken the time and spent a couple hundred dollars on a full background check, I could have easily lost several hundred thousand dollars.

That would have ruined the taste of caviar for the rest of my life!

Who Should You Lend To?

The decision to lend money is a complicated one, with many steps. Before you even vet the deal being offered, it's important to vet the person asking for the loan. No matter how great a potential investment might seem, it's essential that you never get involved with a borrower who has a history of dishonesty or unexplained financial mishaps. No matter how much you are lending, or at what percentage of the value, the risk of loss always exists. When you know the background of the borrower, you decrease the risk of losing your shirt or getting defrauded.

My company and I go through the exercises discussed in this chapter each and every day. We do them for every single loan, whether it's a fifty-thousand-dollar or a million-dollar loan. If we didn't, our money—and that of our investors—would not be adequately protected. We have passed on loans that are worth two, three, even five hundred thousand dollars—loans that looked great on paper—because the borrower did not meet our requirements.

By asking certain questions and following specific rules, we make sure that our investments are protected and that we are making money. For us, thorough vetting is the only way to do business. It allows us to meet our goals in this business of private lending—to make money and to create a network of satisfied quality customers who can refer us to other trustworthy borrowers.

A few key rules that I always follow when vetting potential borrowers: never lend on the houses your borrowers live in; only lend to LLCs, not individuals; and always check the four C's (credit, collateral, capacity, and character).

The Four C's

When evaluating any borrower, you always need to look to the four C's: credit, collateral, capacity, and character.

> *Credit.* A credit report tells you a very important story. It lets you see when people obtained lines of credit, how long they've been active, what types of balances they have, and whether they pay their bills on time. If they have judgments, you'll want

to look at what type of judgments they are. If the judgments are from mortgage companies or other private lenders, that's a pretty big red flag. That's also why it's important for private lenders to record judgments they have against borrowers: it lets the next lender know who the bad apples are. Overall, a credit report can tell you how leveraged a potential borrower is and his/her history of repaying debt.

Collateral. Collateral is the underlying security or the asset—in this case, the piece of real estate the borrower wishes to acquire. If everything else fails, the underlying asset is what you have to ensure your investment is protected. The most important thing about evaluating the collateral is to value it accurately so that you'll be able to recover the amount of your loan if the borrower fails to pay. I'll share more about evaluating a property in chapter 4.

Capacity. Capacity is the borrower's ability to make the interest payments on your loan without relying on the income that may be generated from the property. If something goes wrong or if the project takes longer than it should, will your borrower be able to make those payments? A part-time investor who has a full-time job, for example, probably has the capacity to handle the payments if the project needs additional equity, but someone with limited cash and no other source of income may struggle to pay if the rehab runs into problems.

Character. Character is the linchpin of any transaction because it tells a lot about your potential borrower. When I meet borrowers, I don't ask only about the project. I ask what they do for fun, what makes them tick, and what excites them. I also ask them, "Why real estate?" and "Why this project?" You can learn a lot from getting to know the borrower on a personal level. As I mentioned at the beginning of this chapter, I also always run a background check. This tells you a tremendous amount about borrowers and usually contains things they don't tell you up front.

The four C's exist to help you answer one question: Is this the type of borrower you want to lend to? Move forward with the transaction only if the answer to that question is yes.

Only Lend to Investors

One cardinal rule of private lending is never to lend on the homes in which your clients live. You should only lend to investors.

This rule is so integral to our model that we make borrowers sign an affidavit in our loan documents stating that they do not intend to live in the property. The main reason for this steadfast rule is that the regulatory framework that protects owner-occupied residential properties presents too many problems if the deal goes south. The collateral, as described in the previous section, and your ability to foreclose if necessary are your ultimate protections against principal loss. If the borrower lives in the property, getting your money out by forced sale becomes a much more lengthy, costly, and troublesome process.

When you ask whether borrowers intend to live in the property, you should trust, but always verify. Make sure that the borrowers don't live there and document the fact that they live elsewhere through photos, inspections, and appraisals. Not following this advice can result in a very costly lesson.

In 2011, my company made a $290,000 loan to a married couple in Washington, DC. We verified driver's licenses and checked that the property on which we made the loan was actually an investment, and that they didn't live in the home. We followed every rule that we've set for ourselves.

The borrowers took longer than expected to pay off the loan, and finally, we told them that they needed to either pay us off or refinance the loan. Instead, they filed for bankruptcy.

They claimed to live at the investment property and insisted we had known that all along. In court, in front of the judge, the woman produced two driver's licenses—both with the same issue date, both within Washington, DC, but with two different addresses. One was the one presented when they came to do the loan, and one had been forged to show the property on which we lent.

Fortunately, because of the steps we had taken during the lending process to protect our investment, we were able to demonstrate that the borrowers were attempting to commit fraud. They claimed to be uninformed about borrowing requirements, but the judge didn't buy it. He said, "You may not consider yourselves to be very sophisticated individuals, but you certainly put together a very sophisticated plan to defraud this lender."

My hope in sharing some of my early mistakes with you is that my experience will help you avoid potential headaches. There still may be some pitfalls along the way, but my aim is to point out some of the stumbling blocks you may encounter and help you understand the steps that you can take to protect yourself and your business.

Never Lend to Individuals

If I can save you from repeating that one mistake involving borrowers claiming to be residents, it will be worth the price of this book. One way to make sure that you don't end up inadvertently lending to an owner-occupant is to never make loans to individuals. While it may seem counterintuitive to limit recourse to the assets of a company, I loan only to LLCs. Why? Because LLCs don't live in homes. Individuals do.

I was once approached by a potential client who wanted to borrow $200,000. He lived in a $4 million home, which he was willing to use as collateral, and indicated that he wanted the loan for business purposes. However, the underwriting process showed substantial credit card debt and a lack of liquid capital. Even though the value of the property far outweighed the amount of the loan, I declined to make it because I couldn't see a clear exit strategy with an owner-occupied home, and I concluded that I could end up not getting paid because the borrower lived in the property securing the loan.

Doing all of the things I've outlined to vet borrowers will help you to mitigate your risk so your investment is as safe as possible. But it's not enough to understand who you're lending to. You also need to know what kind of property to invest in. The next chapter will give you vetting guidelines to help you navigate that process.

Chapter 4

WHAT KIND OF PROPERTY TO INVEST IN

Location, Location, Location

Early in 2016, a borrower named Natanyah came to me for a loan. She had perfect credit and lots of money in the bank. She was the ideal borrower.

I said, "Natanyah, I am happy to lend you the $175,000, but I don't think the area you're looking at for this deal is great. I know that as a lender, I'm protected but you should reconsider this location."

She replied, "Jeff, this is the house I want to buy. I can make $30,000 on this house in six months." So, I made the loan.

It was a six-month loan, but Natanyah finished the renovation in four months. And then the property sat on the market for an additional four months, costing her more than $25,000 in profit.

When she finally found a buyer, she made about $2,000 on the transaction—a lot of effort for a small return, but by that time she was just thankful that she didn't end up losing money. I was thankful too, because her ability to pay off the loan in full was contingent upon the sale of the property.

They say there are three principles of real estate: location, location, and . . . location. The property is your collateral for the loan and your safety net. Therefore, knowing what kind of property to lend on and understanding the dynamics of its location are critical components of your success.

Invest in Your Own Backyard

The most common mistake that people make as private lenders is investing in projects that they don't understand or in areas with which they are unfamiliar. That's why I like lending in my own backyard. I know the area that I currently lend in like the back of my hand, and sometimes I understand the value of certain deals better than the appraisers do. I don't believe that if I lived in Los Angeles, I could accurately assess loans in Idaho. It goes back to the truism that real estate, like politics, is local.

Whether you lend on fix-and-flips or buy-and-holds, you need to understand your investment. Remember that the property is the collateral for your loan, and that, in the worst case, you could end up taking possession of it. So, anytime you make a loan, ask yourself, "Would I be willing to own this property?" No guarantees will ever exist when it comes to private lending. However, by understanding who and what you're investing in, you will give yourself the best chance of consistently getting your money back safely and making a profit.

Evaluating deals may be the most important part of becoming a private lender—but it's not the end of the road. Even after you're ready to make a loan, you still need to know how to protect yourself and your investment. In the next chapter, I'll show you how to take each of these steps.

Deciding Whether to Make the Loan

To decide what kind of property to invest in, you will need to follow three steps. First, you must vet the property. Then, you should order your own appraisal. Finally, you will need to scrutinize the contractor.

Vet the Property

The first thing you should do is decide what types of properties you will invest in. You can pick whichever asset class you like—single-family, multifamily, commercial, office, retail, hotel, or special purpose. I recommend focusing on the asset class that you understand best. In my case, I also consider which asset class I can exit from quickly if the economy changes. In most instances, that means single-family homes. These make the most sense when you are starting out because they are the easiest deals to monitor.

Once you have chosen what type of investment to focus on, you will need to track recent and pending sales in the relevant area and review comparable properties, as generally found in an appraisal, for each potential loan you are considering. You'll also need to analyze the number of days comparable properties are staying on the market, so you have a good idea of how long it will take for the property to sell.

After reviewing the property itself, you will want to evaluate the neighborhood in which it is located. Look at things like gentrification and crime trends, and surrounding amenities and services. Is the property near public transportation? Are there good schools in the neighborhood? These are things that buyers look at, so you need to consider them too.

Finally, and this is the most important rule, you will need to physically inspect each property on which you are considering making a loan. With today's technology, fraudulent borrowers can create sophisticated schemes, including creating houses online that don't exist in the real world. You need to confirm through an on-site visit that the property is real and vacant, and that no visible damage exists that hasn't been disclosed. Do your due diligence and drive around the neighborhood in the morning and at night. That will tell you a lot about the property. Learning everything you can about the property and the surrounding area prior to making a loan will help you become an informed investor. It allows you to develop an understanding of the value of the asset that will be the collateral for your loan.

Really Vet the Property

As with almost all lessons worth learning, here is another one that I learned the hard way. One of the first loans I made was to a paralegal from a reputable law firm. He and I met in person, and I liked him and wanted to make the loan, but I needed to see the collateral.

We did drive by the property, but I was busy, and so I broke one of my own rules about inspecting every property before making a loan on it and didn't go inside. I went ahead with the loan based on that one visit. When I went back to the property to meet the borrower after making the loan, I found out the home had been used as a crack house, which meant the interior needed a lot more work than a normally inhabited house would have. My valuation of the property had been too high, and my estimate of the amount of time the flip would take was too low.

Although I did end up getting paid off on this loan eventually, it took a long time. The effort and energy that I had to devote to managing the project weren't worth the small profit I made. As private lenders, we are interested in making safe, consistent returns. This deal didn't provide that! If I had known the property was a crack house to begin with, I never would have lent on it. That very day, I made it my number one rule to always inspect the property, inside and out.

Vet the Appraisal

Once you have decided on a potential property to lend on, you will need to order an appraisal.

An appraisal is an estimate of the property's value, based on what people are paying for similar properties in that area. Appraisals can vary up to 10 percent, so you should be aware that even a good appraisal could be off within that margin.

It is important to order your own appraisal on each property you are considering lending on, rather than relying on one provided by a potential borrower. Appraisal fraud is rampant, so it is essential that you do not accept a third-party appraisal alone. You should choose and develop a relationship with your own appraiser, one you are willing to depend on for property after property. When you order your appraisal, you will want to instruct the appraiser that you're interested only in comparable properties within a close distance to the subject property, generally within three to six blocks, and not those that are two miles away. This ensures that the property is matched with other properties that are actually comparable. Also, be sure to ask your appraiser to note anything distinct or unusual about the property that might make it sell for more or less than other seemingly comparable properties in the vicinity.

Establishing a realistic and reasonable estimate of the value of the property is essential. Once you have a reasonable estimate of the property's value, you can determine a reasonable amount to lend against that value.

Vet the Contractor

Private lending creates a partnership among three people: you, the private lender; the borrower, who should have "skin in the game" in the form of cash or equity; and the contractor.

The contractor becomes a partner because his or her role is to ensure the quality of the work and its timely completion. As the one completing the work, the contractor is the only one who can ensure that the value you think you're going to get is the value you actually receive. Until the renovation of the property is complete, the property can't be sold, and you can't get your money out of the project. The longer the contractor takes to complete the job, the longer you have to wait to make your next loan, and the more strain your borrower will experience as the costs of delay mount.

When it comes to vetting a contractor, you'll first want to verify the contractor's license and make sure it is current. Then you will need to verify that the contractor has insurance and that it, too, is current. Also, make sure that you are added as a loss payee on the insurance, in case something goes wrong. Next, make sure that the contractor's experience is a good match for the specific project. For example, if your borrower is intending to flip a multi-unit building, make sure that your contractor has experience with that particular type of rehab. You should also get references and check them, both by calling individuals and by viewing the contractor's previous work.

As the private lender, you are putting in the most money, and you become the bank. Though all the parties become partners, you have the greatest risk. And, if you're dealing with a borrower who doesn't have as much experience as you do, you may be in the best position to understand how to protect and facilitate the project. As the one with the most capital at risk, you have the greatest incentive to jump in and actively ensure and monitor your investment.

Given the risks, my advice is, when you're starting out, look for manageable deals. As a rule of thumb, that generally means a project with no more than $25,000 in renovations. It's a learning process, so don't bite off more than you can chew. As the lender, you'll need to monitor the process carefully, and if you're out of your depth, you won't be able to help course correct and keep the renovation on schedule.

Now you have looked at the borrower and the property, and you're leaning toward making your first private loan, but you haven't reached your destination yet. You still have to decide what type of loan to make and how to structure it. The next chapter will break this down for you.

Chapter 5

WHEN TO MAKE A LOAN

Money Well Lent

I once lent $1 million to a man on the verge of bankruptcy. His name was Johnson, and when I met him, he was a very successful contractor and real estate developer in Maryland and Washington. Then the Great Recession hit, and Johnson lost everything. He was about to go under when he came across an old, run-down, sixteen-unit apartment building for sale in Washington, DC. It cost $700,000. It was a bargain, but it was also money Johnson didn't have. That was when he came to me.

Johnson wanted to renovate the property, add three more units, and then put the whole building up for rent in six months. The plan sounded ambitious, to say the least, but I'd worked with Johnson before. I trusted his vision and when I evaluated the deal, it just made sense. So I made the loan, and he went straight to work. He spent about $300,000 on renovations and completely fixed up the building. In six months, it was done.

Johnson refinanced the property and rented out the units. That gave him passive cash flow of $10,000 per month *above* his mortgage payment, along with the $1 million in equity he now had in the property. Bankruptcy was no longer on the radar. That project changed Johnson's life, and we both reaped the rewards of it: I made more than $80,000 on this one transaction.

Know Your Loans

Why did I decide to lend $1 million to a man on the verge of bankruptcy? It wasn't just because I liked and trusted Johnson.

I did it because the deal itself made sense. Because of the value of the collateral, I knew that my money would be safe, and while I would normally want a borrower to have more equity in the project, or at least money in the bank to cover cost overruns, I knew that over six months, I would stand to earn $75,000—a 15 percent annualized return. The potential upside made the additional risk worthwhile. And, because I knew Johnson and his track record of successful projects, I felt that the overall risk was mitigated.

As you can see, I looked at a host of factors before making the loan. As you venture into private lending, you'll need to evaluate every aspect of a deal before you lend on it. In fact, deal evaluation is the most important thing you need to master to become a successful private lender. Why? Because it's very easy to lend people money, but it's much more difficult to get paid back. Private lending doesn't come with any guarantees. However, if you know before you lend that your borrower's plan is executable, your chances of successfully collecting on the loan increase substantially.

As a private lender, generally, you will be lending on two major types of deals: fix-and-flip and buy-and-hold. This chapter teaches you how to analyze and underwrite each of these transactions and presents your two main exit-strategy options so that you can make the best lending decision.

Evaluating Fix-and-Flip Deals

Fix-and-flip deals are for borrowers who plan to buy a property, renovate it, and then resell it.

The "secret sauce" to evaluating a fix-and-flip deal is asking the right questions to accurately underwrite the borrower and the property.

Underwrite the Borrower

As outlined in chapter 3, as with all transactions, the first thing you'll need to evaluate for a fix-and-flip deal is the borrower. To underwrite the borrower, you should look at his or her credit and character, as previously discussed. You will also want to examine the borrower's experience and know how much skin he or she has in the game.

Some important questions to ask include the following:

- How many projects has your borrower done, and were they successful?

- Where are those projects located?

- Has he or she ever borrowed privately or from a bank? (If the borrower is a first-timer, this lack of experience is not necessarily a deal breaker, but it means you may want additional protections built into the deal.)

- Does your borrower expect you to fund the entire project, or is he or she planning to invest his or her own resources? It's always better to work with borrowers who are financially invested in the deal.

Underwrite the Property

After you underwrite the borrower, the second step of the deal-evaluation "secret sauce" is underwriting the property and the contractor renovating it. In the previous chapter, I laid out how to vet the property. To underwrite a fix-and-flip property well—whether the deal is a small renovation or a multimillion-dollar overhaul—there are additional things you'll need to check:

- **Pre- and post-rehab value of the property.** Based on the comps, determine what the property is worth now and what it will be worth when the work is complete.

- **Zoning compliance.** Look at the property zoning so you know that your borrowers can build what they intend to build.

- **Accuracy of renovation estimate.** Verify the renovation budget using a third-party contractor.

- **Timeline.** Verify how long it will take the contractor to renovate this property.

- **Likely "on the market" period.** Know about how many days the property will be on the market before it sells.

The bigger the loan, the more important it is to dig deep with these questions. Get as much of this information as you can to help ensure that you are entering into an investment that makes sense and, most importantly, will pay off in the end in accordance with your set timeline.

Exit Strategy: Sell the Property

Before you decide to make the loan, you must have a realistic exit strategy—a plan that allows you to cash out and remove yourself from the investment. If an exit strategy isn't realistic and can't be effectuated, you run the risk that your borrower might never pay off his or her loan. While anything can happen between the time you make the loan and when you get paid, vetting deals for clear and plausible exit strategies exponentially increases your chance of success.

What is the ultimate goal for fix-and-flip deals? The exit strategy here is the sale of the property. Ideally, your borrower will sell the property at a profit and repay your loan with interest. However, in a worst-case scenario, you may have to foreclose on the borrower and sell the property yourself. Therefore, in evaluating the deal, you'll want to understand what obligations you might have to take on in order to get the property into shape to sell.

Evaluate Buy-and-Hold Deals

Buy-and-hold deals are for borrowers who want to fix up a property and hold it for the long term. In buy-and-hold deals, your exit is facilitated by the borrower refinancing with a traditional loan. You make your money when the new mortgage company takes over and the borrower pays off your loan, including the interest. As with fix-and-flip loans, the "secret sauce" of evaluating buy-and-hold deals is underwriting the borrower, the property, and the contractor.

However, because the exit strategy differs in evaluating a buy-and-hold deal, you'll do all the steps required for a fix-and-flip, and then dig a bit deeper. Before you make your loan, you'll need to look at the same things a traditional bank lender would, including the borrower's tax returns and income, to ensure that your borrower will, in fact, qualify for a traditional loan at the end of the term of your loan. It's also generally a good idea to work with a traditional lender from the beginning so the lender can vet the borrower ahead of time, making the transition from your short-term loan to the longer-term financing streamlined and efficient.

Credit Score

To see if buyers will qualify for a traditional loan, you need to evaluate their credit report. This includes their credit score, which can range from 300 to 850. This score is an amalgam of all of a person's credit information, and it indicates whether the buyer is a good or bad risk. Currently, traditional lenders will generally require a score over 680, so this is another item to check to ensure that your buy-and-hold borrower will qualify for traditional credit.

Tax Returns

The second thing to look at is tax returns. In today's world, people need to show income in order to get a loan. Have you verified two years of tax returns? Are they showing income? You can have borrowers sign a Form 4506-T, which authorizes lenders to verify tax returns. Again, by doing so, you will see whether the buy-and-hold borrower will qualify for the end loan.

Exit Strategy: Refinance the Property

We discussed selling the property with fix-and-flip deals. The main exit strategy with buy-and-hold deals is refinancing the property.

When the property is refinanced, a new loan is drafted with another lender at a lower interest rate, usually for a longer period. This new loan is collateralized by the new-and-improved property. Just as you monitor your collateral and every renovation, you need to monitor the refinance process itself to ensure that the borrower successfully repositions and stabilizes the property. Keep in mind that, if the borrower doesn't hold up his or her end of the deal, you may need to consider foreclosure.

In the next chapter, we'll delve more deeply into the nuts and bolts of making a loan. I'll also provide suggestions and insights that will help you build safeguards and best practices into your lending process and protect your investment.

Chapter 6

HOW TO PROTECT YOURSELF AND YOUR INVESTMENT

Beware the Handshake Deal (or how not to make a gift)

In 2010, a guy who had borrowed from me three times in the past came to me with an urgent request for a loan that he needed to close quickly. He sketched out the amounts on a napkin over lunch. He didn't have any funds to invest in the deal himself, but he said it was a great opportunity. And, he said, if I'd provide the capital, he'd handle all of the renovations and the sale, we'd split the proceeds from the sale evenly, and I'd also make 8 percent on the funds I lent him as part of the loan.

Because of the time constraints, I didn't record all of the terms of the deal properly. When it came time to sell the property, the borrower denied that he'd ever agreed to split the proceeds of the sale, and all I had, outside of some very basic documents setting out the 8 percent, was the napkin, which proved unenforceable. So, I lost out on the upside of that deal and put up all of the capital for the deal without adequately pricing in the risk. From that experience, I learned that if you don't put all of the terms of a deal in writing, you should assume that you're making a gift!

Papering the Deal

"Papering the deal" in private lending means you're ready to make the loan, your borrower has accepted the terms you've offered, and it is time to draft the loan documents that reflect the deal to which you've both agreed. To execute this process successfully, you will need to take a few practical steps and protective measures.

It may be tempting to skip some of the due diligence and documentation when there are pressures to make the loan expediently. However, you are more likely to get paid back if you document the loan properly, so resist your urge to cut corners. Remember that, if something goes wrong, proper loan documents may be the only thing that protects your investment. Ultimately, agreements are only as good as the people making them, but you must also make sure your documents are enforceable and recorded as a lien or mortgage at the courthouse. Put everything in writing. Otherwise, you risk leaving your investment unprotected and losing valuable time and money.

In this chapter, I'll explain the steps you need to take to protect yourself and your investment. These steps include understanding the laws of the relevant jurisdiction and your insurance needs, creating loan documents and drafting loan instructions, and recognizing the elements of a successful closing. One of the best ways to protect yourself and your investment is to assemble a top-notch team of professionals you can rely on.

Team of Professionals

Papering your loan is where the rubber meets the road. A real estate closing has a lot of moving parts, and this is where the opportunity for expensive mishaps can occur. That's why, to do it successfully, you need to surround yourself with a team of professionals to support you. In fact, you need a cohort of stellar professionals to support you throughout the cycle of a transaction. The following is a list of professionals you'll want to have on your team and what you should look for when selecting each. Working with these professionals to take care of the technicalities and also to create a friendly atmosphere is the key to a successful transaction.

1. **Appraiser**—As previously discussed, a good and trustworthy appraiser will accurately appraise the property to tell you the value in

its current condition and what it will be worth after the renovation. Make sure that the person you hire is licensed, carries insurance, and can provide references. You might also want to ask the appraiser for some recent appraisals he or she has done and run them by another appraiser for a second opinion. Ideally, you can develop a relationship with one appraiser over time and have someone you can always trust to give you honest assessments.

2. **REALTOR**—A good REALTOR will know the neighborhood in which the property is located and will be able to validate what your borrower is telling you about how likely it is to sell or attract tenants. Values can vary from block to block, and a REALTOR should be tuned in to these nuances. It is helpful to have a handful of agents you can call on when vetting a property, to get different perspectives.

3. **Mortgage lender (for buy-and-holds)**—A licensed and reputable lender who understands the lending business and current trends and programs will be able to help transition your borrower to a permanent loan. Look for someone who has specific experience navigating the transition from short-term hard money loans to

long-term financing. This will help streamline the process. Mortgage lenders can also serve as good resources when vetting exit strategies for buy-and-hold transactions.

4. **Insurance agent**—Find an agent who can offer a comprehensive assessment of all the types of insurance you need for a project and who understands the type of exposure lenders and builders have. If possible, ask other lenders for referrals. Find a reputable agent who has worked with other investors who will be with you for repeat business and will sell you only what you need.

5. **Title company**—Many title companies will know how to work with real estate investors, but make sure to ask about their experience. They should be able to provide you with information that's especially important to an investor, including liens and other red flags that might give a lender pause.

6. **Title insurance company**—Generally, the best source of referrals is your title company, so make sure to ask the company to recommend an insurer.

7. **Real estate lawyer**—Your lawyer will be an incredibly important part of your team. He or she will ensure that your loan documents are enforceable and in accordance with state and local laws. You can also rely on your lawyer for guidance about local laws that may affect your lending terms or the viability of a project.

Understand the Law

Lending laws vary from state to state. To protect your investment, you need to know the laws in the state in which you are making your loan. Some of the most critical aspects of law that you need to understand are the following:

1. **Usury laws**—You'll want to make sure you know what the legal limits are so that you don't overcharge on a loan. Remember that the slightest overcharge can result in hefty fines, so it's important to check all of your terms against the local laws.

2. **Licensing**—In some states, you may be required to obtain a license in order to make loans. Make sure that you check if there are licensing requirements before you begin lending.

3. **Foreclosure laws**—These often differ from state to state, and even county to county, so it is important to understand how onerous the process is in each location where you make a loan.

4. **Landlord/tenant**—You may encounter a situation where a borrower has tenants in a building on which you need to foreclose. Jurisdictions have different laws regarding tenants, so it's important to understand what your options and obligations will be.

5. **Lending laws**—Local lending laws govern fees and many other elements of the transaction, so it is important to understand all applicable laws. Overcharging by $100 could cost you thousands in fines. The best way to learn about the laws in your area is to work with industry professionals and attorneys. Work with your lawyer to ensure that you understand the laws in your state, county, and township. In addition, real estate courses can often provide you with a broader understanding of the relevant laws.

Secure the Right Insurance

Securing appropriate insurance is also an important step in protecting yourself. You must have lender's title insurance for every mortgage, with no exception. Title insurance confirms that you have a "first mortgage" position when the loan is closed, meaning that you will have priority over all other liens or claims on the property in the event of default. It is there to protect you if, for instance, there is any challenge to your borrower's ownership, or your first mortgage position. This protection can save you headaches down the road.

I once had a borrower who signed for a loan but later challenged the validity of her own signature on a technicality regarding the notary who witnessed it. She claimed she didn't have to repay the loan, and that the property was hers, free and clear. The title insurance company stepped in and defended our position, saving us $30,000 in legal fees. Eventually the borrower repaid the loan. So, while you might be tempted to try to save costs on insurance, it is never a good idea to leave yourself exposed.

In addition to title insurance, I personally require builder's risk insurance for any loans that include a renovation component. It protects materials, fixtures, and equipment used in the construction and renovation of a building. One of my borrowers, who was renovating a four-unit property in a high-crime area, had a break-in during the project.

Four sets of kitchen appliances were stolen. Even with this unfortunate event, the project remained on budget because the builder's risk insurance covered the cost of replacing all four sets. You may also want to consider a commercial general liability insurance policy. This protects you, the borrower, and the contractor if someone gets hurt on the job at the borrower's property.

It is also absolutely crucial that you make sure your borrower meets your requirement for property insurance, pays the premium, and lists you on the policy as the loss payee. Then, in the event of a loss, the money doesn't go solely to the borrower, allowing him or her to take the insurance proceeds. This policy ensures that the money will be used to restore the property and that you will have access to it.

Insurance policies differ from location to location. Talk to an insurance expert to make sure you're getting the right coverage for all aspects of your loan. Make sure that your policy covers your entire loan!

Setting Up Loan Documents and Instructions

To protect yourself and your investment, you will need a strong set of loan documents. Like the laws, and often because of them, these documents vary from state to state, but they cover essentially the same things: the collateral and security for the loan, the loan terms, the interest rate, and the loan's final maturity, or date due. Loan documents should include the monthly payment amount and due dates and should state whether you're creating an interest reserve—a special savings account funded out of the proceeds of the construction loan, from which the interest is paid. The documents should also note what will happen in the event of a default, a zoning violation, or (God forbid) the death of the borrower. Each of these terms should be agreed upon by you and the borrower before you draft the documents.

Another important aspect of protecting your investment is drafting good loan instructions. Loan instructions are exactly what they sound like—instructions to the closing agent from you or your attorney. They cover everything, including the property's address, loan amount, rate of interest, points and fees being charged, due date of the loan, and who is to be paid from the loan proceeds. In addition, all of your requirements for the title company or closing agent should be outlined in the instructions. They should also indicate whether you are escrowing funds for interest, taxes, and insurance. Just as an architect draws the design for a building, the loan instructions draw the outline of the loan from top to bottom.

Your lawyer will be an especially important resource when it comes to setting up loan documents and instructions, so make sure that you have hired someone who practices real estate law in your geographic area for this stage.

As mentioned before, the stronger your loan documents and instructions are, the safer you'll be.

Elements of a Successful Close

Once you've leveraged your professional team and have covered all of your bases, you are ready to move forward to paper your loan. To successfully close your loan, you'll need to review the property's title report, get a land survey and a closing protection letter, and continue to work closely with your team of professionals.

Title Reports

A title report will provide you with decades' worth of information about the title of the property. This allows you to see what happened in the chain, or history, of the title and should include the owner of record, previous owners, previous transfers, liens on the property, current taxes owed, attorney judgments against the current owner, and more. Although the report contains a tremendous amount of information, you may need to do further digging for more details or insight. For example, study what the property sold for before and what it's selling for now. These details will give you a better understanding of the property's value and ensure that nothing, such as judgments from previous owners or unpaid taxes or liens, affects your borrower's title claim.

Land Survey

The land survey is generally ordered by the title company and performed by a land surveyor. It is a drawing of the property on which you are lending, including land measurements and artificial structures. It identifies the boundaries of the collateral and allows you to confirm them. If there are a lot of changes noted on the land survey, investigate further to make sure everything is recorded properly.

Once, I was almost ready to make a loan to a borrower, but after checking the survey, I determined that there was a dispute about the bounds of the property and that the neighbor actually held the title and the legitimate claim. The loan eventually closed, but it took four months to get the neighbor to grant an easement and allow the project to begin. I was glad to have discovered the issue before tying up my capital for that period.

Closing Protection Letter

The closing protection letter is issued by the title insurance agency. While the letter states many things, its most important statement is that the lender will be compensated by the closing agent for loss resulting from agent misconduct. This covers such circumstances as a title agency being guilty of fraud or dishonesty in handling the money or documents at closing or failing to follow certain written closing instructions.

One Success Leads to Another

Remember that at the closing table, you're still selling your ability to deliver the product and meet the needs of your borrower. One success encourages others. Make it a point to leave a positive impression with your borrower every time you close on a loan. As a private lender, your success depends, in large part, on having satisfied customers.

Of course, making the loan is one thing, but actually getting the return on your investment is another. In the next chapter, I'll discuss how to achieve the end goal of your project: getting paid.

Chapter 7

How to Get Paid

The Right Process

I once made a $200,000 loan to a woman named Dorothy who wanted to buy, renovate, and then hold a four-unit building in her real estate portfolio. My systems were solid. My team performed all of the due diligence in advance, making sure to underwrite Dorothy, her income, her credit, and all other components of the deal. I also made sure that I had a process in place to ensure that I would be able to exit the deal after the renovation of the property was complete. I identified a lender that was willing to handle the refinance and reviewed her tax returns to ensure she earned enough to qualify for the traditional loan that ultimately replaced mine, so that when the time came, she was able to refinance without any difficulties.

Dorothy was successful. In six months, she had renovated, rented, and refinanced the property. She paid me back on time—again, thanks to the systems I have in place—and I made $20,000 on that deal. Because I underwrote according to the exit strategy—a buy-and-hold, versus a fix-and-flip—this loan went smoothly, and I was able to get paid and exit the deal. I have found that the more you stick to a meticulous, proven process, the easier it is to get paid. It's also essential to make sure that the process you employ facilitates the specific exit strategy appropriate for each deal.

Get Paid

Getting paid as a private lender boils down to three things: loan servicing, loan monitoring, and loan payoff. I've provided some basic best practices to help you get through to your payday.

Loan Servicing

Loan servicing is how you collect interest, principal, and escrow payments from the borrower. This involves ensuring that you have streamlined processes and procedures you set up, so that you are able to take the same care with each loan. You also need to have regular, timely communication with your borrower, so that all of the payments and expectations are clear.

Loan Monitoring

Loan monitoring is how you track your borrower's finances—usually via financial statements, tax returns, or credit reports. It also includes frequent property inspections to ensure the renovations are being done within budget and on schedule and that they are of good quality. It's especially important to monitor projects to ensure that the funds are, in fact, being used to renovate the properties, so that the collateral increases in value as you disperse the funds.

Loan Payoff

A loan payoff is when the transaction wraps up. Ultimately, as private lenders, we make money only when our loans pay off. And, as I've said, it's often very easy to loan money, but it can be very difficult to collect it. As part of the lending and repayment process, it's important to focus on not only loan servicing and monitoring until the end of the loan's term, but also the execution of your exit strategy.

In this chapter, we will also discuss the main parts of servicing and monitoring a loan, including verifying permits, loan extensions, the debt service coverage ratio (DSCR), and loan payoff strategies.

Verify Permits

It's tempting to assume that your borrower will have verified that the project is viable, but it's always best to check for yourself. In order to ensure that what your borrower wants to build can be done legally, you need to verify that building permits have been issued.

In 2007, for one of my first loans, I had a borrower who wanted to renovate a large single-family home and turn it into a four-unit building. I visited the house, thought that the project had merit, and decided to make the loan. In the course of monitoring the process, I discovered that the borrower's certificate of occupancy only allowed him to renovate the property as a two-unit home. This transition from a four-unit property to a two-unit property decreased the property's value, hurting both my borrower and me. From this experience, I learned that something as seemingly small as a permit can have an enormous impact on the ultimate value of a property.

To avoid this situation, as part of your regular lending process, you should require every borrower to furnish copies of the building permits needed. Do your research to verify those permits, and also check your borrower's plans against your area's zoning regulations to make sure that there are no conflicts and that the proposed changes to the property will, in fact, be legal. Otherwise, your collateral may be worth less than you originally calculated, leaving you in a tough spot if the borrower defaults.

Loan Extensions

A loan extension is an increase in the amount of time you allow your borrower to repay his or her loan. As you continue to monitor and service your loans, you will encounter a certain number of extension requests. Before granting an extension, you'll need to do two things.

First, you'll need to determine whether the reason for the delay is reasonable. Making this determination usually involves inspecting the property and meeting with the borrower to discuss the delays that are preventing him or her from sticking to the agreed-upon schedule. Things like permitting-related delays, reasonable changes to the scope of work on the property, or a short-term delay in securing long-term financing would all likely be valid reasons to grant an extension. But if the borrower's project is poorly run, or if there are unexplained cost overruns or indications of financial mismanagement, you might consider declining the request, demanding a payoff of the loan and beginning collections. If you are comfortable with the cause of the delay, you'll then need to determine a realistic new timeline for payoff.

Second, you'll need to decide whether you will charge a fee for the extension. You make money only when you deploy your capital. It is industry practice to make borrowers pay a fee for extending their use of your capital. Banks charge fees for extensions on their loans; thus, in most circumstances, it is totally acceptable for private lenders to do the same. As a lender, you can view these fees as an additional return on your investment. As a general rule, I need to cover my opportunity costs when I won't be able to redeploy my capital. However, I also consider my total return on the loan, the overall relationship with the borrower, and the length of the extension request. Sometimes I will grant the extension and charge less than I'm entitled to, simply to maintain customer satisfaction and end a loan on a high note. This tends to pay off in repeat business and referrals.

Though extensions often make sense, there are times when you will determine that it is not prudent to give a borrower more time. If I conclude that the property will not be worth enough to pay off the loan, or if the borrower is not current on insurance or other obligations, I will generally decline the extension request. In those circumstances, a lender generally has two options. The first is to take possession of the property, either by getting a deed in lieu, in which the borrower agrees to turn over the deed to be released from the remaining loan obligation or by foreclosing on the borrower and taking over the property. The second is to force the borrower to refinance elsewhere and pay off the outstanding loan to you. Both of these options can bring additional challenges, so it's important to think through each strategy.

When working to get a deed in lieu, you need to present a clear case to the borrower, demonstrating that it makes more financial sense to surrender the property to avoid potential judgments and collections for many years to follow. If you take this route or proceed to foreclosure, you will need to be ready to take on completing the project or selling the property as is, which may result in a loss. Whichever path you choose, it's important to understand what the implications will be. If you decide to try to get another lender involved, be aware that the new lender may have some of the same concerns, but there may be more patient capital that can provide relief.

Borrowers in a Jam

Seemingly reasonable people can do unreasonable things when they find themselves in a jam. I once had a borrower who just couldn't complete his project on time. I'd already given him several extensions, adding up to twelve months. One day, I finally informed him that I'd given him his last extension. If he did not complete the project by the next deadline, I would begin foreclosure.

He seemed to understand. But the next day, he filed for bankruptcy. It turned out that he had spent most of the money I had lent him without finishing the project. I proceeded with foreclosure and took over finishing the project, but it delayed the sale by eighteen months, and

I had to spend an additional $35,000 of my own funds to complete the project. Eventually, after the sale, I recovered all of the principal, but I didn't earn any interest on this transaction, meaning that I effectively lost money in making the loan, and I spent countless hours fixing a problem that shouldn't have happened.

Scenarios like this should be few and far between, but it's important that you know when to push back and say no. When it comes to getting paid and making the most of your original loan, you need to look for red flags early on that might point to a potential failure. In my case, this borrower's project had a long construction process and delay after delay. Instead of continuing to extend his loan, I should have done my due diligence and acted more quickly on my concerns.

The Debt Service Coverage Ratio (DSCR)

The DSCR represents the relationship of a property's annual net operating income to its annual principal and interest payments (aka debt service). Why is this important? Imagine your borrower purchases and renovates a property to fix and flip but then finds that he can't sell it right away. In that case, he might rent it to a third party to stabilize the investment. When the borrower stabilizes the investment using this strategy, you need to be certain that the property is making enough money to cover the loan and interest payments.

Understanding the DSCR is important when you're monitoring a loan, especially with a buy-and-hold property. Understood another way, the DSCR notes the percentage of a mortgage that is covered by a tenant's rent payments.

For example, if the debt service, or mortgage payment—including principal, interest, and any escrow, as well as taxes and insurance—on your loan is $3,000, and your borrower's total monthly income from the property is $3,000, that's a 1.0 rating, or a 1.0-to-1.0 ratio. To make a profit, you'll want to see a 1.25 to 1.35 rating. This rating means that the income is covering an extra 25 percent or 35 percent beyond the mortgage payment, which indicates that the borrower will have ample income to cover the debt service.

In order to have greater certainty that the debt service is covered, your borrower could also set up a triple net lease, an arrangement under which the tenant pays all real estate taxes, building insurance, and maintenance (the three "nets") on the property in addition to routine fees such as rent and utilities. The higher the DSCR, the more likely it is that both you and your borrower will get paid and that the property will make money, so it's important to think through how much the borrower will be able to charge for a property that he or she intends to buy and hold.

Payoffs

A payoff is just what it sounds like. When you receive a payoff, your borrower has paid off your loan.

It may seem that a payoff would be simple, but it actually involves a number of steps, including a review of the terms of the loan and any extensions made and a final calculation, because it's easy to lose track of all payments owed. To ensure that the payoff for your borrower's loan is correct, I suggest meeting with your accountant and/or bookkeeper to review the accuracy of your calculations for any interest, points, fees, and advances due. It's always good to have a second set of eyes to ensure you're collecting everything you've earned.

To start the payoff process, a title company will typically send the lender a "payoff request," which should include the loan's scheduled closing date and where the funds are to be sent. You may charge the borrower interest, or a per diem, should the closing date need to be extended. Once you receive the funds to pay off the loan in full, you will execute a release of the loan, and the title company will close it out by entering the mortgage satisfaction in the title record.

A Few Steps Closer to Payday

The steps laid out in this book are the key components of a private loan, and they are all aimed at ensuring that your investment pays off. By doing your due diligence and monitoring and servicing your loan correctly, you are building processes that help insulate you from discoverable issues and challenges along the way, while protecting healthy returns. At this point, you have a clear overview of how to find, vet, structure, and earn a return as a private lender. The next chapter will tie everything together and discuss what you can do to keep growing your private lending venture.

Chapter 8

THE NEXT HORIZON

The Rewards of Private Lending

In 2008, just after the market crash, a woman named Pamela came to me for a loan of $180,000 to buy and flip a house. She had assessed that the renovations would cost $40,000 and that she'd be able to sell the property for $300,000. The deal seemed to make sense, and Pamela was a postal worker with good credit and money in the bank, but because of the more stringent bank regulations that had emerged after the Great Recession, she couldn't get financing.

When she came to me, she was frustrated because she felt that she was missing out on an opportunity to increase her savings. I agreed that she had identified a solid opportunity, and I lent her the money. Pamela successfully flipped and sold the house and paid back the loan. Over the next several years, she found more opportunities. Each time she came to me, I made the loan and she completed the project, making a profit for herself as well as for me.

This is what I love most about my work. Many of my borrowers have been people who had the capacity to follow through on lucrative projects but were unable to secure the financing they needed, especially after the market crash. This was a time when many distressed properties were available for cents on the dollar. I feel fortunate that I've been able to make a living by giving these borrowers the means to enhance their own income by providing them with an opportunity that they weren't able to access from traditional lenders.

It's a privilege to partner with these entrepreneurial people. When a borrower finalizes a sale on a flipped property, paying off the loan while pocketing a profit, there is always a sense of pride and satisfaction in having seized and capitalized on an opportunity. I get to share in that, often repeatedly with the same borrower over time. Other types of investments can feel impersonal. But if you become a successful private lender, you have the pleasure of doing well when your borrowers do, and of financing projects that will benefit them as well as you.

A Look Back

Now that you've read through this book, you have a basic map and tools to help you begin your own private lending journey. You've learned about the benefits of private lending and different platforms and avenues for making your first loan or expanding your lending activities if you already have some experience. You've considered different risk profiles and ways to mitigate risk in your lending profile, and I've provided insights to help you select the right types of investments and to effectively underwrite your borrowers and vet the projects they propose. We've also covered recommendations for papering your loan effectively and pulling together a team of professionals to help protect your investment and ensure your success. Finally, we've reviewed exit strategies for two main types of projects and options and considerations when borrowers request extensions on their loans. Now that you have this road map, you're ready to get started making your own loans.

Moving Forward

Private lending is an evolving industry. And success in an evolving industry requires flexibility. As I've discussed in previous chapters, private lending doesn't come with any guarantees, but your best strategy for protecting yourself and your investment is to make sure that you have a complete understanding of all of the components of the loans you make. These components include the trustworthiness of the borrower; the nature, location, and condition of the underlying property; and the quality and experience of the professionals involved, from the contractor to the team you assemble to support you in papering the loan. It also includes the regulatory environment in which you and your borrower are operating, where everything from zoning and permits to laws regulating lending practices can have a significant impact on your returns. Fortunately, you now have a list of considerations and supports that you'll need to help you along the way.

Next Steps

The good news as you get started is that there are many avenues, some of which were discussed in chapter 1, to venture into private lending, and many experienced professionals to support you if you decide to develop a portfolio of loans, either through a self-directed IRA or by launching your own private lending firm. There are also conferences and resources such as the National Private Lending Institute that provide opportunities for networking and learning about the industry. My experience has shown me that people in this space are generous with their time and experience, so it's worthwhile to attend an event or two so that you can make connections and learn more, even if you're just curious or just starting out in private lending.

For your first loans, you may want to invest through an online platform or partner or place your funds with a more experienced lender. As you gain confidence and continue to learn through conferences, seminars, courses, and industry professionals, your confidence will grow, and you'll be able to manage larger loans and projects effectively.

I wish you success in your private lending journey and hope that my experience and advice will prove useful to those considering entering this space. The rewards of earning a living while helping support borrowers in achieving their goals, especially when other lenders can't or won't help, are considerable. If you're like me, you'll find that the collaboration and successes through partnership with your borrowers are as rewarding as the financial gains of the industry. Good luck, and enjoy this opportunity!

GLOSSARY

Acceleration Clause: A clause in a mortgage or deed of trust that advances the due date of the debt upon a breach of the contract. These are frequently found in private-money commercial loans.

Additional Principal Payment: A payment by a borrower in excess of the scheduled principal amount due in order to reduce the remaining balance on the loan.

Advances: Payment of funds by a lender to a borrower of monies already borrowed. Advances are made when all of the borrowed money is not extended at the time that the loan is closed.

After Repair Value (ARV): The value that the investment property is expected to be worth after the planned renovations are complete.

All Inclusive Deed of Trust: A new deed of trust that includes the balance due on the existing note plus new funds advanced. It is also known as a wrap-around mortgage.

Amortization: The gradual reduction of a loan balance, generally made in regular payments over a specified period of time. Payments are typically made to cover interest and principal. Many private money loans will typically be interest only because they are for a shorter duration than bank loans.

Amortization Schedule: A table showing the breakdown of amortized loan payments into principal and interest portions and the remaining loan balance after each payment.

Annual Percentage Rate (APR): The cost of credit, including points and fees, on a yearly basis, expressed as a percentage.

Application Fee: A fee charged by a private lender to submit an application.

Appraisal: A professional assessment of how much a piece of real estate is currently worth or will be worth after a renovation.

Arrears: An overdue debt caused by a missed payment.

Assessor's Parcel Number (APN): Number used by the tax assessor to identify a parcel of land.

As-is Value: The value of a property as it currently exists legally and physically, as of the effective date of the appraisal. It is the value of the property before renovations are undertaken.

Assignee: Person to whom rights to a property, title, or other interest are transferred.

Assignment: Document transferring rights to a property, title, or other interest from one person to another.

Automated Valuation Model (AVM): A method of calculating a property's value using mathematical modelling combined with a database.

Bad Boy Clause: A clause that gives personal liability to the borrower and principals of borrower upon the occurrence of certain *bad* acts (fraud) committed by the borrower or its principals.

Balloon Loan: A loan that does not amortize, and for which the principal is due at the end of the loan term.

Balloon Payment: A large lump-sum payment that is due at a specified period of time during the course of a mortgage loan, usually at the end. A balloon payment may be for all or some of the loan amount and will generally be specified in the promissory note.

Bankruptcy: A proceeding authorized by federal law that provides debtors with various kinds of relief from their debts.

Beneficiary Demand: An estoppel letter from the lender to the borrower that explains exactly what is required to be released from a debt.

Beneficiary's Statement: A statement from the lender of record that discloses the unpaid balance remaining on a mortgage loan as of a certain date, including the interest rate.

Blended Interest Rate: An interest rate charged on a loan that represents the combination of two interest rates, often a first mortgage and a second mortgage. For example, a $200,000 loan at 6% and a $50,000 junior lien at 8.5% would yield a blended rate of 6.5% ($16,250 of combined annual interest / $250,000 loan balance).

Bridge Loan: A short-term loan used until permanent financing is secured or an existing obligation is removed (property sold or refinanced and the lien satisfied). This type of financing allows a borrower to meet current obligations.

Broker Price Opinion (BPO): A property valuation by a licensed real estate broker that results in a written evaluation of the property and the estimated value.

Capitalization Rate (Cap Rate): The ratio of Net Operating Income (NOI) to property asset value. For example, if a property recently sold for $1,000,000 and had an NOI of $100,000, then the cap rate would be $100,000/$1,000,000, or 10%.

Chapter 13 Bankruptcy: A reorganization of a borrower's debts. Chapter 13 of Title 11 of the United States

Bankruptcy Code allows individuals to undergo a financial reorganization that frequently gives a borrower three to five years to repay its debts including a mortgage.

Chapter 11 Bankruptcy: A reorganization that is found in Title 11 of the US Bankruptcy Code. A Chapter 11 bankruptcy is similar to a Chapter 13 bankruptcy but is filed by businesses such as LLCs and corporations.

Chapter 7 Bankruptcy: A bankruptcy that does not involve filing a plan of reorganization like a Chapter 13 or Chapter 11 bankruptcy. In a Chapter 7 bankruptcy, a court-ordered trustee liquidates (sells) all assets owned by a debtor in order to pay creditors.

Consumer Financial Protection Bureau (**CFPB**): An agency of the United States government responsible for consumer protection in the financial sector. CFPB jurisdiction includes banks, credit unions, securities firms, payday lenders, foreclosure relief services, debt collectors, and other financial companies operating in the United States. As of the date of this publication, the CFPB does not regulate private lenders.

Closing: Also known as the settlement, the Closing is often the final step in a real estate transaction. It is when all necessary documents are executed to facilitate either the refinance or transfer of the subject property. It also includes the execution of loan documents by the borrower.

Closing Costs: Costs paid at closing for loan origination and processing, including attorneys' fees, fees for preparing and filing a mortgage, fees for a title search, and state and local transfer taxes.

Co-signer/Co-borrower: An additional person who signs the loan documents and assumes responsibility for the payments and the loan liability.

Collateral: For real estate loans, the collateral is the real property used to secure the loan.

Collection: A process that the loan goes into when payment on a loan is delinquent and efforts are made to collect the amount due.

Combined Loan to Value (CLTV): The sum of all liens on the property divided by the value of the property.

Commercial Use: Property that is used for business purposes and has no consumer component.

Conventional Loan: A type of mortgage that is *not* offered or secured by a government entity, like the Federal Housing Administration (FHA), US Department of Veterans Affairs (VA), or US Department of Agriculture (USDA) Rural Housing Service, but rather is available through a private entity like a bank, credit union, or mortgage company or the two government-sponsored enterprises, the Federal National Mortgage Association (Fannie Mae) and Federal Home Loan Mortgage Corporation (Freddie Mac).

Corporation: A legal entity in which individual owners are not directly responsible for debt incurred by the company. In corporations, independent stockholders own parts of the company, but the corporation is its own "person," and its stockholders are not directly responsible for the actions of the company.

Credit Bureau: A company that collects information relating to the credit ratings of individuals and makes it available to credit card companies, financial institutions, and other lenders. Private money lenders are typically more interested in the components of the loan and amount of equity in the collateral than in a credit score.

Credit Report: A detailed report of an individual or company's credit history. Credit bureaus collect information and create credit reports based on that information, and lenders use the reports along with other details to determine loan applicants' credit worthiness.

Credit Score: A number, based on information in your credit report, that is used by most lenders to decide whether to extend credit and at what cost. The most common score used is called a FICO score.

Creditor: A person or business from whom you borrow or to whom you owe money.

Cross Collateralize: A lending technique when an asset or assets are used as additional collateral for a loan.

Crowdfunding: A group of investors (who don't necessarily know each other) buy a percentage interest in a loan or property through a single portal.

Debt Consolidation: Refinancing one or more existing debts into a new loan. In the mortgage-lending context, relatively short-term, unsecured debt is often rolled into a long-term mortgage loan.

Debt Service Coverage Ratio (DSCR): A measure of the cash flow available to pay current debt obligations. In private lending, it is expressed as percentage. The DSCR is calculated by dividing net operating income (NOI) by debt service. For example, for a property with $50,000 of annual rent and an annual debt service of $40,000, the DSCR would be 1.25%.

Debt-to-Income (DTI) Ratio: The amount of money you pay out each month as a percent of your gross income. For example, $2,500 of monthly debt service/$5,000 of gross income = 50% DTI ratio.

Default: Default on a loan is when a borrower fails to comply with any of the terms of an agreed-upon loan, including timely repayment.

Default Interest Rate: A higher interest rate that is imposed on a borrower when there is a breach of the loan terms, such as when the borrower is in default.

Depreciation: Loss of value in real property brought about by age, physical deterioration, or functional/economical obsolescence.

Dodd–Frank: The Dodd–Frank Wall Street Reform and Consumer Protection Act is financial reform legislation passed by the Obama administration in 2010 as a response to the financial crisis of 2008. This act brought significant changes to financial regulation in the United States.

Draw Schedule: A detailed payment plan for construction or renovation projects. This schedule helps lenders and borrowers determine when they are going to distribute funds to the contractor as the work is completed.

Equal Credit Opportunity Act (ECOA): A federal law that prohibits lenders from discriminating on the basis of race, color, religion, national origin, age, sex, marital status, or receipt of income from public assistance programs or the exercise of certain consumer rights.

Equity: The difference between the fair market value of real property and any outstanding loans, liens, and encumbrances. Private lenders require substantially more equity than banks, credit unions, and other lending institutions.

Escrow: A separate account where money and/or documents are held by a third party until agreed-upon terms and conditions are met. After the terms and conditions are met, the funds are released from escrow. An escrow is an independent neutral account by which interests of all parties are protected.

Escrow Company: A company that oversees the execution of real estate transactions to include closing documents, disbursement of funds, and the recording of documents at county offices. Also known as a Settlement Services Company.

Estoppel Certificate: A document used in real estate to verify facts on a property including rents, leases, mortgage balances, and monthly payments.

Exit Strategy: How the borrower plans to pay off the loan, as well as turn a profit. Having a clear and realistic exit strategy is one of the most important parts of developing your overall plan for a loan.

Fair Credit Reporting Act (FCRA): A federal consumer protection law that regulates the disclosure of consumer credit reports and establishes procedures for correcting errors that may appear on a credit report. Private lenders do not generally report to credit bureaus.

Fair Market Value (FMV): The value of a property, which is typically based on comparable sales ("comps") of similar properties within the last six months.

FICO Score: A credit score developed by Fair Isaac & Co. that determines the likelihood that credit users will pay their bills. Scoring is widely accepted by lenders as a reliable means of credit evaluation. It is not used by private money lenders as much as by banks.

Financing Costs: The total amount charged to a borrower to borrow funds.

Fixed-Rate Loan: A loan in which the interest rate or scheduled principal and interest payment amount does not change during the term of the loan.

Forced Place Insurance: Property insurance placed on a property by a private lender in the event that a borrower allows its insurance coverage to lapse. The cost is advanced by the lender and added to the balance of the loan.

Foreclosure: The legal process by which an owner's right to real property is terminated, typically due to a default. Each state and jurisdiction has its own foreclosure process.

Foreclosure Fees: Costs incurred by a private lender to foreclose on a property. These costs are added to the balance of the loan.

Fractionalized Loan: A single loan funded by two or more investors. Private money loans are often fractionalized to reduce the amount of funds required by any one investor.

Full Recourse Loan: A loan in which the lender is entitled to pursue the borrower's other assets if the debt is not fully satisfied by the collateral.

Guarantor: A person who agrees to assume individual responsibility for any amounts borrowed from a private lender.

Hard Money Lender: A lender that makes private money loans. Funds typically come from the lender's personal account or are raised from private investors.

Hard Money Loan: A loan typically secured by a hard asset such as residential or commercial real estate. Such loans usually have higher interest rates than bank loans. Hard money lenders typically look more to asset value than at the credit characteristics of the potential borrower as the primary loan underwriting factor. Hard money lending is useful to those who are in need of quick financing, since these loans can be closed in as little as a few days.

Holdback: Portion of a construction loan amount that is not released until a certain stage (such as completion of the foundation) is reached.

Holding Costs: Costs attributed to owning an investment property for a period of time. This includes interest payments, property taxes, maintenance, insurance, and utilities.

HUD-1: A standard government real estate form that is used by the settlement agent (also called the closing agent) to itemize charges imposed upon a borrower and seller for a real estate transaction.

Improved Value: The value of a piece of real estate after the property is renovated.

Interest Rate: The amount that a borrower has agreed to pay a lender as the price of borrowing a sum of money expressed as a percentage. If the interest rate is 10% for one year on a $100,000 loan, the borrower will pay $10,000 for the use of money for one year. ($100,000 × 0.1 = 10,000).

Internal Rate of Return (IRR): The rate of return on an investment that considers positive and negative cash flows over a specific period of time.

Junior Lien: A lien against a property that is subordinate to another lien. It is not in first priority or position. Private lenders generally do not offer junior liens.

Late Fee: A fee paid by a borrower if a loan payment is not made on time.

Lender: A private, public, or institutional entity that makes funds available for others to borrow.

Lien: A form of security interest. It is a legal claim related to a piece of property to secure the payment of a debt or performance of some other obligation.

Limited Personal Guarantee: A guarantee that sets a dollar amount owed by borrowers in the event a borrower defaults on a loan. Limited guarantees are often used when multiple business partners take out a loan.

Limited Liability Company (LLC): A corporate entity that protects individual members from financial liability in excess of the amount a member has invested.

Loan Officer: An individual who help borrowers get a loan.

Loan to Value (LTV): A ratio derived from the formula (Loan Amount)/(Appraisal Value). This is a number expressed as a percentage.

Maturity Date: The date by which a debt or loan is to be repaid.

Nationwide Mortgage Licensing System (NMLS): The NMLS identification number is the unique identifier assigned to registered Mortgage Loan Officers. In some states, private lenders must have a NMLS number.

Multiple Listing Service (MLS): A database in which real estate for sale is listed for a given area or region. Real estate brokers from this area work together to compile this list.

Mortgage: A legal agreement by which a lender lends money at interest in exchange for taking title of the debtor's property, with the condition that the conveyance of title becomes void upon the payment of the debt.

Net Operating Income (NOI): The result of gross operating income less operating costs. NOI equals all revenue from the property minus all operating expenses.

Non-Recourse Loan: A loan in which the lender is not entitled to pursue the borrower's other assets owned if the debt is not fully satisfied by the collateral in the event of foreclosure and re-sale of the property.

Note: An abbreviation for "promissory note." A note is a signed document containing a written promise to pay a stated sum to a specified lender on a specified date.

Payoff: The act of paying off a loan by paying the outstanding principal amount and additional interest and/or costs due to completely satisfy the loan obligation.

Payoff Statement: A statement that provides information on the amount of money required to pay off a loan.

Personal Guarantee: An individual's legal promise to repay charges to a lender. By providing a personal guarantee, an individual legally agrees that if the business or LLC becomes unable to repay its debts, the individual guarantor is personally responsible for those debts.

Points: Finance charges paid to a lender at closing. Each point equals 1% of the loan amount. Some lenders charge a flat fee, rather than points. For example, 1 point on a $100,000 loan is the equivalent to $1,000.

Prepayment Penalty: A clause in a mortgage contract stating that a *penalty* will be assessed if the mortgage is prepaid within a certain time period. The *penalty* can be based on a percentage of the remaining mortgage balance or a certain number of months' worth of interest. For example, a private lender who originates a loan might say that the loan must stay out for three months; if the loan is repaid in two months, there would be a one-month interest pre-payment penalty.

Principal Balance: The outstanding balance of principal on a loan, which does not include interest or other charges.

Private Lender: A non-institutional individual, group of individuals, or company that lends money that is generally secured by a note and deed of trust for the purpose of funding a real estate transaction. They usually lend their own funds and are considered a nontraditional source of lending.

Promissory Note: A legal document that sets out a borrower's obligation to pay a debt at agreed-upon terms. Frequently abbreviated to "note."

Proof of Funds: A document prepared by a private lender and sent to a borrower that is intended to document that a borrower has the available funds to complete a transaction. A bank statement can also be a proof of funds.

Property Flipping: Buying and then renovating a property in order to increase the value of the asset such that it may be sold at a profit.

Protective Advances: Payment of funds by a private lender for something that was supposed to have been paid for by the borrower or for services required to protect the collateral.

Purchase Price: The cost to acquire the property.

Real Estate Investor: Someone who purchases properties with the intent to make a profit, either by holding the asset for rental income or reselling it at a premium to cost.

Referral Fee: A fee paid by a private lender to someone, such as a mortgage broker, for referring a borrower.

Refinance: Replacing an existing loan with a new one. Typically, people refinance to get a lower interest rate on their loan and/or to leverage real estate value for cash. Refinancing can be an exit strategy for borrowers that have private loans.

Relief of Stay: Court-granted relief from the automatic stay of collection actions against a debtor in a bankruptcy filing. This allows a creditor to proceed with collection and/or foreclosure actions.

Renewal Fee: A fee paid by a borrower to renew an existing loan for an additional term.

Renovation: The process by which a property is renewed, restored, or modernized.

Real Estate Owned (REO): The foreclosure property repossessed by banks or private lenders. If a lender or bank is the highest bidder at a foreclosure auction—or if no third party bids at the auction—the property is sold to the lender and becomes REO.

Return on Investment (ROI): A performance measure of the amount of return on an investment relative to the investment's cost. This is a percentage derived from the formula: (Net Profit/Cost of Investment) × 100. For example, if your net profit is $100,000 and your investment costs are $300,000, your ROI would (0.33) × 100 = 33%.

Scope of Work: An outline of renovations scheduled to be completed before a property is sold or refinanced, as well as their anticipated costs. The scope of work can also provide a timetable of when the property will be complete.

Second Mortgage: A lien on a property that is junior to a first mortgage. Private lenders can offer second mortgages, but they are less secure than first mortgages.

Secured Loan: A loan for which security is provided by the borrower. Security is provided by something of value that serves as collateral for the loan. In private lending, the security is the real estate.

Self-directed IRA: An individual retirement account in which a custodian handles alternative investments at the direction of the account owner. This custodian enables private lenders to make private money loans from their retirement accounts.

Servicer: A company that handles payment-related transactions with borrowers, including accepting monthly payments, issuing monthly statements, providing year-end tax statements, and paying property taxes and insurance when due.

Settlement Services Company: A company that oversees the execution of real estate transactions to include closing documents, disbursement of funds, and recording of documents at county offices. Also known as an Escrow Company.

Short Sale: This occurs when a seller is selling its property for less than it owes on its mortgage. For this to happen, the bank or lending company needs to approve the sale at the lower price. Short sales are a popular way to find investment properties because of their lower purchase prices.

"Skin in the Game": A phrase used in private lending that indicates how much money a borrower or borrowers have in a particular real estate transaction.

Stabilized Value: The value of a property after it reaches stabilized occupancy.

Stay: The automatic prohibition of collection actions against a debtor in a bankruptcy filing.

Takeout Loan: A loan that replaces a short-term or bridge loan.

Time Value of Money: A core financial principle stating that money is worth more the sooner it is received.

Title: The evidence of the right to ownership of real property.

Title Company: A company that searches county and public records for liens and encumbrances against a subject property and the borrower. It provides a preliminary title report and an offer of title insurance that is based on the report. It issues title insurance at transaction settlement.

Title Insurance: A form of indemnity insurance that insures against financial loss from defects in title to real property and from the invalidity or unenforceability of mortgage loans. There are two types of policies: one insures the owner for losses, and one insures the lender for losses.

Traditional Financing: A loan secured through a financial institution under conventional terms, usually based on the "four Cs": character, collateral, capital, and capacity. The process for securing such financing is fairly standardized, with lenders looking at your credit history, business plan, and assets when assessing your qualifications. Traditional financing is used in private lending when the borrower wants to have longer-term financing and hold a property for a longer term.

Trust Deed: A security instrument that secures the promissory note to real property and is recorded in the county land records as evidence of the debt.

Underwriting: The process of assessing of risk and reward for a potential investment. Underwriters assess the credibility of a potential investor and determine if its investment is going to perform.

Unlimited Personal Guarantee: A guarantee by a borrower to a lender for 100% of outstanding loan amount plus legal fees, accrued interest, and costs associated with collecting the loan. This type of guarantee entitles the lender to look to the borrower's personal assets to recover any unrealized balance due if the foreclosure and re-sale of the asset do not satisfy the debt.

Usury: The illegal practice of lending money at unreasonably high rates of interest. *Usury* is usually carried out with the intention of the lender, or usurer, gaining an unfair profit from the loan. Usury rates vary from state to state.

About the Author

Jeff Levin is the president and CEO of Specialty Lending Group and Pinewood Financial (collectively "SLG")—one of the most successful private-lending platforms in the country. A sought-after speaker and market expert on real estate investing, Levin has generated thousands of loans, originated more than $300 million in loan volume, and overseen $1.5 billion in total loan production. Through SLG, Levin shares with investors around the world his proven process for how to safely and profitably engage in private lending.

With more than twenty-five years in the business, Levin offers great insight into an aged yet evolving industry. He specializes in sharing his expertise with novice and seasoned investors alike in an easily digestible manner. Levin serves on the Education Advisory Committee of the American Association of Private Lenders (APPL) and as the Learning Chair of the Washington chapter of the Entrepreneurs Organization. He has also served on the advisory board of a $1 billion FDIC-insured bank, as well as on the board of directors of the mid-Atlantic chapter of CCIM.

Levin believes that you only get out of life what you put into it. By sharing his knowledge and industry expertise with others, he hopes to create something bigger than himself. Levin lives on Capitol Hill in Washington, DC with his wife, Dunnzy, and their two sons.

Private Lending 101

Ready to become a private lender?

The National Private Lending Institute (NPLI) offers understandable education for both new and experienced private lenders. Our workshops and seminars teach you how to:

- Lend to people you can trust
- Find deals that pay—consistently
- Protect yourself with a proven loan process
- Safely earn above market returns

NPLI also offers the industry-accepted Accredited Private Lender (APL) designation, so you can distinguish yourself as a credible private lender.

NPLI hosts dozens of educational seminars and workshops throughout the country. To find an event near you, visit our website: www.nplinstitute.com

EARNING THE APL DESIGNATION

Elevate yourself from the crowd by earning the distinguishing Accredited Private Lender (APL) designation. The APL curriculum provides everything you need to be a successful private lender—allowing you to be a leader in your market.

Following your successful completion of the course, you will know how to:

› Structure your business to succeed in any market;
› Recognize a bad deal while you can still walk away;
› Cut through appraisals and credit reports and identify exactly to whom you should lend;
› Use the proper documentation to protect you and your clients; and
› Calculate payoffs to earn healthy, safe, and consistent returns.

Increase your knowledge and proficiency while simultaneously unlocking enormous opportunities to expand your career and your business. Obtaining your APL designation will allow you to:

› Gain the trust of your clients;
› Distinguish yourself in an ever-increasing market;
› Access the best industry-specific education; and
› Join the expanding network of private lenders.

For more information, visit our website: WWW.NPLINSTITUTE.ORG

NPLI is a proud partner of the American Association of Private Lenders (AAPL)

READY TO BECOME A PRIVATE LENDER?

NPLI

NATIONAL PRIVATE LENDING INSTITUTE

When you're ready, **WWW.NPLINSTITUTE.COM** is the place to start! The National Private Lending Institute (NPLI) offers you the educational resources to begin your journey into private lending. Read our blog, download our resources, or find an event near you. Take the step to begin your journey by obtaining your Accredited Private Lender (APL) designation.

NPLI is a proud partner of the American Association of Private Lenders (AAPL)

IS PRIVATE LENDING RIGHT FOR YOU?

- ☑ *Would you like to earn safe and consistent returns investing in a growing market?*

- ☑ *Do you want to diversify your retirement portfolio to capitalize on expanded private lending opportunities?*

- ☑ *Are you interested in deploying your capital profitably, while helping others succeed?*

- ☑ *Would you like to be able to deploy capital at short intervals for healthy returns, without tying it up for long periods?*

Find out how the APL designation through NPLI can help you get there.

———— **WWW.NPLINSTITUTE.COM** ————

NPLI is a proud partner of the AAPL

Jeff Levin is a speaker, author, and private lending expert who has completed over $1 billion in originations. He has trained thousands of people on how to earn safe and consistent returns through private lending. He is a frequent guest speaker and panelist who uses his decades of industry experience to teach others about a side of real estate many haven't considered.

Create opportunities for your audience and have Jeff speak at your next conference or Real Estate Investors Association (REIA) event. To submit requests or learn more about Jeff, visit him at **www.JeffLevinLends.com.**

Jeff's track record demonstrates a real expertise in earning excess returns.

Craig Peterman, CFA, CFP,
Managing Director, Prism Wealth Management

Jeff is a key player in the private lending space and is someone to listen to.

Anthony Geraci, Esq., Geraci Law Firm

I highly recommend Jeff for anyone who currently invests in real estate or for those who are looking for a better way to deploy their money.

Todd Reeber, CPA

40516697R00073

Made in the USA
Middletown, DE
27 March 2019